KONSTANT KASH

Bitcoin Utopia:
The Global Financial Revolution You Can't Afford to Ignore

First published by PC House Productions, Inc. 2024

Copyright © 2024 by Konstant Kash

All rights reserved. No part of this publication may be reproduced, stored or transmitted in any form or by any means, electronic, mechanical, photocopying, recording, scanning, or otherwise without written permission from the publisher. It is illegal to copy this book, post it to a website, or distribute it by any other means without permission.

First edition

*This book was professionally typeset on Reedsy.
Find out more at reedsy.com*

To My Children
Kyah, Cooper, Savannah, Jordan
"Fly You Fools" ~Gandalf

Contents

Introduction	1
Bitcoin: A Catalyst for Global Financial Inclusion and Prosperity	1
1 The Rise of Bitcoin and Its Impact on Global Finance	3
Satoshi Nakamoto and the Birth of Bitcoin	3
Bitcoin's Divisibility and Role as Money	5
What Makes Something "Money"?	6
How Bitcoin Fulfills the Role of Money	7
Bitcoin as Both Medium of Exchange and Store of Value	8
Bitcoin's Role in the Global Economy	9
Understanding Blockchain, Decentralization, and Bitcoin's Unhackable Ledger	9
The Challenge of Duplicating Bitcoin's Network	12
Bitcoin's Unique Approach to Conserving Energy	13
Why Transparency and Security Matter	13
The Bitcoin Network: A Global, Always-On Financial System	17
A Digital Future: How Bitcoin Reflects the Shift in Global Finance	18
Bitcoin as a Hedge Against Instability	19
The Long-Term Impact of Bitcoin on Global Finance	20

Bitcoin Is Not a Passing Trend	21
2 Bitcoin vs. Gold: A New Standard for Storing Value	22
Storage and Portability	22
Supply and Scarcity	24
Tokenization and Trust	26
Network Anonymity and Decentralization	30
The New Era of Digital Sound Money	31
3 Bitcoin vs. The US Dollar	32
The Declining Buying Power of the US Dollar	32
The Rise of the US Dollar as the Global Reserve Currency	33
The Dollar's Declining Status and the Rise of Alternatives	34
The Bitcoin Comparison: A Hedge Against Dollar Debasement	36
A Likely Scenario: Dollar Inflation, Bitcoin Integration	37
The Future of Bitcoin in the Global Economy	38
4 The Global Unbanked Crisis – Bitcoin as a Solution to...	41
The Reality of the Unbanked	41
The Failure of Traditional Financial Systems to Serve the Poor	43
Bitcoin and Decentralized Finance: A New Path to Financial Inclusion	43
Real-World Impact: Case Studies in Financial Stability	44
Bitcoin's Role in Reducing Financial Barriers	45
The Growing Wealth Gap: Traditional Banking's Role in Economic Inequality	46
Bitcoin: Leveling the Financial Playing Field	46

    Bitcoin as a Shield Against Corruption   48
    Bitcoin as a Tool for Financial Sovereignty   48
5 The Halving Cycle and the Future of Mining: Sustaining...   50
    The Four-Year Halving Cycle and Bitcoin Mining   50
    The Role of Miners in the Bitcoin Network   51
    Post-2140: What Happens After All Bitcoin is Mined?   53
    Comparing Bitcoin's Mining Costs with Traditional Finance   54
    The Future: A More Efficient Global Financial System   56
    Bitcoin's Place in the Evolving Financial Landscape   57
6 Bitcoin as Conserved Monetary Energy   59
    Understanding Conserved Monetary Energy   59
    How Bitcoin Mirrors Technological Advances in Energy Conservation   62
    Bitcoin's Role in Reducing Monetary Friction   63
    Traditional Banking vs. Bitcoin's Energy Efficiency   64
    A Future with More Efficient Financial Energy   66
    A Greener Future for Global Finance   67
7 Historical Examples of Energy Conservation Driving...   68
    Agriculture: From Hand Labor to Mechanized Farming   68
    Manufacturing: The Rise of Automation   69
    Transportation: The Internal Combustion Engine and Global Supply Chains   70
    Energy: The Shift from Fossil Fuels to Renewables   70
    Communications: The Internet Revolution   71
    Bitcoin's Parallels with Energy Conservation   72

8 Bitcoin, Transparency, and the Global Financial System	73
The Problem with Traditional Financial Transparency	73
Bitcoin's Transparent Blockchain Solution	75
Real-World Applications of Bitcoin Transparency	76
Global Implications: From Financial Trust to Peace	77
A New Era of Accountability	78
Bitcoin's Potential as a Catalyst for Global Peace	79
Fostering Global Collaboration and the Creative Economy	81
A Transparent Path Forward	82
9 Conclusion – A Future Powered by Bitcoin	83
Bitcoin's Role in Shaping the Future of Finance	83
Bitcoin Utopia: A Decentralized Global Network	84
Bitcoin as a Borrowing Asset	85
A Global Network for Everyone	86
Earning Through Engagement	87
Government and Corporate Transparency on the Blockchain	92
Politicians Held Accountable by a Transparent Financial System	92
Opening Access to Global Investment Through Tokenized Assets	93
Bitcoin and Generational Wealth	95
Bitcoin: A Foundation for Global Prosperity	96
A Limited Supply in an Expanding World: Securing Your Share of the Future	99

Introduction

Bitcoin: A Catalyst for Global Financial Inclusion and Prosperity

Bitcoin has emerged as one of the most revolutionary innovations of the 21st century, reshaping how we think about money, value, and finance. Its decentralized nature offers a peer-to-peer network that operates independently of traditional banks and governments. This is particularly significant in a world where over 1.4 billion people remain unbanked, with no access to basic financial services like bank accounts, credit, and savings.

But why is the discussion around Bitcoin so urgent now? In 2024, institutional investments from major players like BlackRock and Fidelity skyrocketed, with Bitcoin-focused exchange-traded funds (ETFs) holding billions in assets. Bitcoin is no longer just a speculative investment; it is rapidly becoming the bedrock of a new financial system. For the unbanked, it offers a revolutionary lifeline to financial inclusion, and for investors in wealthier nations, it provides a hedge against inflation and economic instability.

This book explores how Bitcoin is reshaping the global financial landscape and how its potential extends far beyond being an asset class. It dives into how Bitcoin could address systemic global issues like financial exclusion, transparency, and energy conservation, providing a path to a more prosperous future for all.

1

The Rise of Bitcoin and Its Impact on Global Finance

Satoshi Nakamoto and the Birth of Bitcoin

In 2008, amidst a global financial crisis, an anonymous figure (or group) using the pseudonym Satoshi Nakamoto published the now-famous whitepaper, *"Bitcoin: A Peer-to-Peer Electronic Cash System."* This groundbreaking document introduced the world to Bitcoin, a decentralized digital currency that fundamentally challenges traditional financial systems and the way we understand money itself.

Bitcoin wasn't just a new form of currency; it was a direct response to the failures of centralized financial institutions. The 2008 financial crisis exposed the fragility of banks and governments, leading to widespread unemployment, loss of homes, and economic despair across the globe. Traditional financial institutions, operating under systems of trust, had overleveraged themselves and failed, leaving millions to bear the consequences. Nakamoto envisioned a financial system that would bypass these intermediaries entirely, giving individuals the ability to transfer value without relying on banks, governments, or third-party institutions that had proven to be fallible.

But perhaps the most revolutionary aspect of Bitcoin is that Satoshi created and then released this algorithm into the world with no central entity in control. No person, company, or government can dictate its protocol or manipulate its supply. Bitcoin is an autonomous, self-sustaining form of money, engineered to operate without the need for any central authority. This autonomy is what sets Bitcoin apart from all forms of currency that preceded it. It is governed solely by its code, ensuring that it remains decentralized and immutable.

Bitcoin represented a fundamental shift in financial power, placing control directly into the hands of individuals in a decentralized, trustless system. At the core of this system is the blockchain—a public, distributed ledger of transactions that offers transparency and security never before seen in traditional finance. This innovation paved the way for a new era in which people could own and transfer money without needing to place their trust in any central authority.

100 Million Satoshis Per Bitcoin

Bitcoin's Divisibility and Role as Money

Despite Bitcoin's capped supply of 21 million coins, its divisibility ensures its scalability as a global currency. Each Bitcoin (BTC) can be divided into 100 million smaller units known as Satoshis. This divisibility ensures that even as Bitcoin's value increases over time, it can still be used for everyday transactions, from buying a cup of coffee to conducting large international trade.

For example, 1 Bitcoin (BTC) = 100,000,000 Satoshis, and 1 Satoshi = 0.00000001 BTC. As Bitcoin's value rises, people will simply transact in smaller units, maintaining its utility across different scales of trade. This flexibility makes Bitcoin practical in a global financial ecosystem, regardless of its future price.

What Makes Something "Money"?

To understand Bitcoin's role in the global financial system, we must first define what constitutes money. Economists typically agree on several key attributes that any form of money must have:

1. **Divisibility**: The currency must be divisible into smaller units to accommodate transactions of varying sizes.
2. **Durability**: Money must be durable, able to retain its value without degrading over time.
3. **Portability**: Money needs to be easily transferred across distances, physically or digitally.
4. **Fungibility**: Each unit of money must be interchangeable with any other unit of the same value.
5. **Scarcity**: The supply of money must be limited to maintain its value over time.
6. **Recognizability**: People must easily recognize and verify the currency.
7. **Store of Value**: Money must preserve its value over time, allowing individuals to save and accumulate wealth.

How Bitcoin Fulfills the Role of Money

- **Divisibility:** Bitcoin is divisible into 100 million Satoshis, allowing it to facilitate both microtransactions and large-scale exchanges. This divisibility is critical as Bitcoin's value increases, enabling users to transact in smaller fractions for everyday purchases and large business deals alike.
- **Durability:** Unlike physical forms of money, such as paper bills or coins that degrade over time, Bitcoin is entirely digital and does not face physical wear and tear. Its ledger, the blockchain, preserves the history and integrity of every transaction indefinitely, ensuring Bitcoin's durability as a form of money.
- **Portability:** Bitcoin can be transferred across borders instantly, making it far more portable than physical forms of money or gold. Regardless of the amount, whether $10 or $10 million, Bitcoin transactions occur with the same efficiency, enabling global trade and financial transfers to happen without the limitations imposed by traditional banking systems or physical transport.
- **Fungibility:** Each Bitcoin, or fraction of a Bitcoin, is interchangeable with another. This is crucial for any currency to function effectively. In the case of Bitcoin, fungibility ensures that every unit of Bitcoin has equal value and can be used in trade without issues of differentiation, which is critical for its use as a medium of exchange.
- **Scarcity:** Bitcoin's scarcity is perhaps its most defining feature. Unlike fiat currencies, which can be printed by central banks at will, only 21 million Bitcoins will ever exist. This hard-coded limit into Bitcoin's protocol makes it immune to inflationary pressures caused by an ever-

expanding supply. Bitcoin's fixed supply guarantees that its value will be preserved over time, much like gold.
- **Recognizability:** Bitcoin has gained increasing recognition as a legitimate form of currency. With the proliferation of Bitcoin ATMs, exchanges, and merchant acceptance, people around the world can easily recognize and verify Bitcoin's value through open blockchain data. As more businesses and institutions adopt Bitcoin, its global recognizability will continue to expand.
- **Store of Value:** As a store of value, Bitcoin's fixed supply and decentralized nature make it a strong hedge against inflation and currency devaluation. In times of economic uncertainty, Bitcoin has become an alternative to fiat currencies, much like gold, offering individuals a means to preserve and accumulate wealth outside the influence of governments or central banks.

Bitcoin as Both Medium of Exchange and Store of Value

Bitcoin serves a dual function, both as a **medium of exchange** and a **store of value**, two critical functions of money.

- **Medium of Exchange**: Bitcoin is increasingly used for daily transactions. Its acceptance by major companies such as Tesla, Microsoft, and PayPal, as well as its integration into retail payment systems, has solidified Bitcoin's role as a legitimate medium of exchange. Online platforms, as well as merchants globally, now offer Bitcoin as a payment option, enabling consumers to use it for purchasing goods and services.

- **Store of Value**: Bitcoin's scarcity and resistance to inflation make it a secure way to store wealth. Many see Bitcoin as "digital gold" due to its ability to retain value over time, especially as fiat currencies suffer from inflationary pressures. This role has only been strengthened as global economic instability has led more people to seek alternatives to traditional assets and currencies.

Bitcoin's Role in the Global Economy

Given Bitcoin's inherent qualities—such as divisibility, portability, and scarcity—it is becoming an increasingly significant player in the global economy. Its decentralized nature offers a viable alternative to traditional financial systems, which are often burdened by inefficiencies, fees, and centralization. As businesses, institutions, and individuals continue to recognize Bitcoin's potential as both a medium of exchange and a store of value, it becomes evident that Bitcoin is more than a speculative investment—it is a contender for the future of global finance.

Understanding Blockchain, Decentralization, and Bitcoin's Unhackable Ledger

At the heart of Bitcoin's revolutionary design is the **blockchain**, which acts as a public, decentralized ledger where every Bitcoin transaction is recorded and verified. Unlike traditional financial systems, where centralized institutions like banks or governments control the ledger, Bitcoin's blockchain is maintained by a distributed global network of computers (nodes). This decentralized structure ensures that no single entity can manipulate or control the system, providing unparalleled security and transparency.

Bitcoin's decentralized architecture makes it virtually unhackable. Each transaction must be verified by thousands of independent nodes through a consensus mechanism called **proof-of-work**. This system prevents bad actors from altering the ledger, as doing so would require controlling more than half of the network's total computational power—an almost impossible task given Bitcoin's global scale. Once a transaction is recorded on the blockchain, it becomes an immutable part of the ledger, unable to be altered or reversed.

The Bitcoin Network is Unhackable

But beyond its decentralized architecture, Bitcoin's network is a remarkable demonstration of transparency on a global scale. Every transaction is publicly verifiable, allowing anyone to audit the ledger in real time. This transparency, combined with the inability to alter past transactions, creates a level of accountability that traditional systems simply cannot match.

The Challenge of Duplicating Bitcoin's Network

Critics argue that the Bitcoin Network could be replicated by another type of cryptocurrency. However, such a notion fails to account for the vast amount of infrastructure that has been developed around Bitcoin over more than a decade. The Bitcoin Network is secured by a massive global network of miners who use specialized hardware to validate transactions and secure the blockchain. These miners have collectively invested billions of dollars in equipment, energy, and infrastructure to maintain the network's integrity.

To illustrate the scale of this investment: as of 2023, the global Bitcoin mining industry is estimated to have reached over $20 billion in annual revenue, with many large mining operations spread across various countries, utilizing cutting-edge hardware and innovative energy solutions . These operations are supported by data centers, cooling systems, and power plants, many of which are custom-built specifically for Bitcoin mining. In fact, some nation-states and large corporations have begun to monetize surplus energy, such as flared gas from oil fields or renewable energy from solar and wind farms, specifically for Bitcoin mining.

For another cryptocurrency to replicate Bitcoin's infrastructure, it would not only require a similar level of financial investment but also new energy monetization strategies. This is no small feat. Bitcoin's miners have spent years fine-tuning their operations, and replacing such a globally entrenched system with a new cryptocurrency would render these enormous investments obsolete—a highly unlikely scenario.

Bitcoin's Unique Approach to Conserving Energy

Bitcoin's **Proof of Work (PoW)** algorithm is often criticized for being energy-intensive. However, this energy consumption is essential to secure the network and prevent fraudulent transactions. PoW transforms computational power into a system of cryptographic security, ensuring the integrity of Bitcoin's blockchain. While alternative consensus mechanisms, such as Proof of Stake (PoS), claim to be more energy-efficient, none have demonstrated the same level of security, decentralization, and transparency as Bitcoin's PoW model.

Additionally, the energy used in Bitcoin mining has driven innovation. Many miners have turned to renewable energy sources and innovative energy-saving technologies. In some cases, Bitcoin mining has incentivized the development of renewable energy infrastructure or allowed miners to monetize wasted energy that would otherwise go unused. This evolving landscape highlights how Bitcoin is adapting to energy concerns while maintaining its unmatched level of security.

Why Transparency and Security Matter

Traditional financial systems are built on a foundation of trust. We trust banks to safeguard our money, governments to issue stable currencies, and financial institutions to facilitate transactions and manage our assets with integrity. However, history has repeatedly shown that this trust can be misplaced. Banks can collapse due to mismanagement or risky practices, leading to the loss of deposits or savings. Governments can devalue their own currencies through inflationary policies or economic manipulation, eroding the purchasing power of citizens. Financial institutions can also fall victim to corruption, fraud, or incompetence, further undermining the integrity of the global financial system.

These systemic risks are exacerbated by the opaque nature of traditional financial systems. The inner workings of banks, governments, and financial institutions are often hidden from public view, making it difficult for individuals to verify the security or soundness of their assets. For instance, when a bank operates under a fractional reserve system, customers have no way of knowing how much of their deposited money is actually held in reserve or how much is being used for lending or speculative activities. This lack of transparency leaves individuals vulnerable to institutional failures, and when trust is broken, the consequences can be devastating.

Bitcoin represents a radical departure from this trust-based model by replacing human trust with cryptographic proof. Instead of relying on centralized entities to manage and secure transactions, Bitcoin operates on a decentralized network where every transaction is verified by a distributed network of nodes. This process, known as **proof-of-work**, ensures that each transaction is mathematically validated and recorded on an open, immutable ledger—the blockchain. This cryptographic verification process removes the need for trust in intermediaries, as every transaction can be independently verified by anyone with access to the Bitcoin network.

The decentralized nature of Bitcoin is central to its transparency. Unlike traditional financial systems, where transactions are hidden behind layers of institutional control, Bitcoin operates on a fully transparent public ledger. Every transaction ever made on the Bitcoin network is permanently recorded and publicly accessible. This means that anyone, anywhere, can verify the validity of a transaction in real-time, ensuring that the system is accountable and free from manipulation. By decentralizing the verification process, Bitcoin eliminates the risk of institutional bias, corruption, or human error, providing a level of security that far exceeds that of traditional financial systems.

Moreover, Bitcoin's transparency goes beyond just transaction verification. Its monetary policy is encoded in the network's protocol and is known to everyone. The total supply of Bitcoin is capped at 21 million, and the issuance schedule—how many new bitcoins are minted and when—is predetermined and cannot be altered. This is in stark contrast to fiat currencies, where central banks have the authority to print more money at will, often leading to inflation and devaluation. In Bitcoin's case, the rules governing supply are fixed and transparent, giving users the confidence that their holdings will not be subject to inflationary manipulation by any central authority.

Bitcoin's security is also bolstered by the **decentralization of power**. In traditional financial systems, a centralized entity like a bank or government holds the authority to freeze accounts, reverse transactions, or seize assets, often without the consent of the individual. This centralized control leaves users at the mercy of these institutions, especially in regions where governments or financial systems are corrupt or unstable. In contrast, Bitcoin operates in a peer-to-peer network, meaning no single entity controls the system. Once a Bitcoin transaction is confirmed, it cannot be reversed or tampered with by any authority. This gives users full control over their funds, shielding them from external interference.

The network's resilience is another key aspect of its security. Bitcoin is maintained by a global network of miners who expend computational power to secure the blockchain through the proof-of-work mechanism. This vast, decentralized network of nodes ensures that the system is incredibly difficult to attack. For a bad actor to successfully compromise Bitcoin, they would need to control more than 50% of the network's total computational power, an extremely costly and unlikely scenario given the global scale and participation of the network. This makes Bitcoin resistant to censorship, fraud, and other forms of malicious interference, ensuring the integrity of the system for all users.

In addition to its robust security, Bitcoin provides **unprecedented financial sovereignty**. In traditional systems, individuals are often dependent on third parties to access, manage, and protect their wealth. A bank failure, a government-imposed capital control, or a fraudulent intermediary can quickly strip individuals of their assets. Bitcoin, by contrast, allows users to take full custody of their wealth. Private keys—long strings of cryptographic data—are the only means by which a user can access their bitcoins, and they are solely controlled by the user. As long as a user maintains control of their private keys, no one else, including governments or institutions, can access or confiscate their funds.

Bitcoin's transparency and security are not just theoretical benefits—they are actively reshaping how people view and interact with money, particularly in regions where traditional financial systems have failed. In countries experiencing hyperinflation, currency devaluation, or government corruption, Bitcoin has provided a lifeline, allowing individuals to preserve their wealth in a system that is transparent, secure, and free from the whims of centralized power.

In conclusion, the transparency and security of Bitcoin represent a significant leap forward from the trust-based model of traditional finance. By operating on cryptographic proof and decentralizing the verification process, Bitcoin provides a financial system that is not only more secure but also more transparent, empowering individuals with control over their assets and eliminating the need to place blind trust in intermediaries. In a world where financial uncertainty is growing, Bitcoin offers a stable, secure, and transparent alternative to the vulnerabilities of traditional financial institutions.

The Bitcoin Network: A Global, Always-On Financial System

One of Bitcoin's most revolutionary features is its ability to operate 24/7, 365 days a year. Traditional banks and financial institutions operate on strict schedules, often closing on weekends and holidays. In contrast, Bitcoin is always available. Whether it's the middle of the night or a national holiday, Bitcoin transactions can still be made, verified, and recorded on the blockchain.

This constant availability is a game-changer. For businesses operating in multiple time zones or for families sending emergency funds across borders, Bitcoin offers unparalleled speed and efficiency. There are no delays due to bank closures or bureaucratic processes—transactions happen instantly, giving users full control over their finances at any time.

A Digital Future: How Bitcoin Reflects the Shift in Global Finance

The world is moving toward a digital future. Just as the internet revolutionized industries like retail and communications, Bitcoin is doing the same for finance. The rise of e-commerce has shown how digital platforms can displace traditional models—online shopping now accounts for a significant portion of global retail sales, and this trend continues to grow.

Bitcoin fits perfectly into this digital transformation. Like e-commerce, it offers a financial system that is borderless, digital, and efficient. Traditional financial institutions are weighed down by physical infrastructure, regulations, and operating hours, but Bitcoin bypasses these limitations, providing a solution tailored to the needs of a global, digital economy.

Bitcoin as a Hedge Against Instability

Fiat currencies are controlled by governments and central banks, which can print money as needed. While this allows flexibility, it also introduces the risk of inflation. As more money enters circulation, the value of each unit decreases, eroding people's savings. In extreme cases, like Venezuela and Zimbabwe, hyperinflation has rendered national currencies nearly worthless.

Bitcoin offers a solution. Its supply is capped at 21 million coins, meaning no central authority can inflate its value by producing more. This scarcity makes Bitcoin an attractive store of value, especially in economies plagued by instability. People in countries with collapsing currencies have turned to Bitcoin to protect their savings from devaluation, using it as a safe haven when traditional currencies fail.

The Long-Term Impact of Bitcoin on Global Finance

Bitcoin's impact on the global financial system is only beginning to be realized. By removing intermediaries like banks and governments, Bitcoin empowers individuals to take control of their financial futures in ways that were previously unimaginable. Its decentralized, transparent, and secure system disrupts traditional power structures that have historically controlled the flow of money. Bitcoin isn't just a technological innovation; it's a profound shift in how we think about money, ownership, and financial autonomy.

As Bitcoin continues to gain adoption worldwide, it's likely that traditional financial institutions will need to adapt or face the risk of obsolescence. The inefficiencies, costs, and limitations of the current system—such as slow international transfers, high transaction fees, and reliance on third parties—are being challenged by Bitcoin's more efficient, decentralized model.

The future of finance is digital, global, and decentralized, and Bitcoin is leading the charge. This shift could have far-reaching implications for global trade, individual wealth preservation, and economic stability. As businesses, governments, and individuals come to recognize the advantages of decentralized finance, Bitcoin may increasingly become the backbone of a new financial system—one that is open to all, not controlled by a select few.

Bitcoin represents more than just an alternative currency—it's a symbol of financial freedom, resilience, and the future of money in a digital world. As we look ahead, Bitcoin has the potential to transform not only how we store and transfer value but also how we interact with and understand the very concept of money itself.

Bitcoin Is Not a Passing Trend

Bitcoin's rise is a testament to its ability to challenge the status quo in global finance. From its creation in response to the failures of traditional financial systems to its divisibility and ability to function as a store of value, Bitcoin demonstrates the characteristics of a modern, decentralized currency fit for a digital age. Its transparent, secure, and always-on network presents a compelling case for a future where individuals, not institutions, hold the power over their financial lives.

As more people and institutions adopt Bitcoin, it's becoming clear that this digital currency is not a passing trend. Bitcoin has the potential to reshape the global economy, offering an inclusive, efficient, and decentralized financial system that transcends borders and traditional power structures. By addressing the flaws of current financial models and empowering individuals around the world, Bitcoin stands poised to become a cornerstone of the future of finance.

2

Bitcoin vs. Gold: A New Standard for Storing Value

For centuries, gold has been considered a reliable store of monetary value. Its rarity and physical properties have made it a popular hedge against inflation and economic instability. However, in the digital age, Bitcoin has emerged as a new standard for storing and transferring value, offering advantages over gold in several key areas.

Storage and Portability

One of the main differences between gold and Bitcoin lies in the cost and logistics of storage. Gold, being a physical asset, requires secure storage facilities, such as vaults, and often insurance. These storage costs can add up, especially for large quantities. Furthermore, transporting gold is a cumbersome and expensive process. Moving significant amounts of gold internationally involves logistics companies, security measures, and legal compliance, making it a slow and costly endeavor.

Bitcoin, by contrast, exists entirely in the digital realm. It can be stored on a hardware wallet, computer, or even memorized through a seed phrase, with minimal cost. Bitcoin can be transferred across borders almost instantly and with a relatively low fee, regardless of the amount being moved. This makes Bitcoin significantly more portable and affordable to store than gold.

Bitcoin is Cheaper and Easier to Store

Supply and Scarcity

One of the most significant distinctions between Bitcoin and gold lies in their respective supply dynamics and scarcity. While gold is often thought of as a rare and precious metal, its supply is not truly finite. New gold deposits continue to be discovered, and mining operations regularly introduce additional gold into circulation. The Earth's vast unexplored areas, such as deep-sea deposits, still hold unknown quantities of gold, which may one day become accessible. Additionally, the possibility of asteroid mining presents a theoretical future scenario in which extraterrestrial gold could flood the market. Any such large-scale discovery or technological advancement could drastically increase the supply of gold, potentially destabilizing its value and reducing its scarcity.

Moreover, the historical supply of gold has not remained constant. Over time, advances in mining technology have enabled more efficient extraction methods, gradually increasing the rate at which gold enters circulation. This slow but steady expansion of supply can impact gold's long-term value, making it less predictable as a store of wealth. Unlike Bitcoin, whose supply is transparent and fixed, the supply of gold is subject to human intervention, discovery, and technological innovation, which could disrupt its perceived rarity.

In contrast, Bitcoin's supply is mathematically finite and immutable. Capped at 21 million bitcoins, this limit is hard-coded into Bitcoin's underlying protocol and cannot be changed without overwhelming consensus from the network—a scenario so improbable that Bitcoin's supply is effectively fixed for eternity.

This enforced scarcity gives Bitcoin a unique and unparalleled quality as a digital asset. Unlike gold, no matter how much demand grows, the supply of Bitcoin cannot increase to meet it. This guarantees that Bitcoin is not vulnerable to inflationary pressures from additional supply, ensuring that its value is preserved by a known and finite quantity.

Bitcoin's scarcity becomes even more pronounced when you consider the mechanics of its issuance. The process of mining Bitcoin follows a predictable schedule, with block rewards halving approximately every four years—a mechanism known as the Bitcoin halving cycle. This gradual reduction in the rate at which new bitcoins are produced ensures that the supply grows more slowly over time, ultimately ceasing entirely when the 21 million cap is reached around the year 2140. As each halving event reduces the number of new bitcoins entering the market, Bitcoin's inflation rate continues to fall, reinforcing its deflationary nature.

This contrast in supply dynamics between Bitcoin and gold creates a divergence in how both assets respond to changes in demand. If demand for gold increases, its supply can eventually expand to meet that demand, even if it takes years or decades. Bitcoin, however, cannot respond with increased production, meaning that rising demand is met with only a static or shrinking supply, which could result in significant upward pressure on its price. This quality makes Bitcoin a unique hedge against inflation, offering protection from the dilution of purchasing power that often accompanies fiat currencies and more abundant resources like gold.

Furthermore, while gold's physical nature makes it susceptible to issues such as storage costs, transportation challenges, and the need for verification, Bitcoin's digital form eliminates these concerns. Bitcoin can be transferred quickly across borders, stored securely in a digital wallet, and easily verified via the blockchain. This gives Bitcoin an advantage in terms of liquidity and portability, while gold, despite its historical use as a store of value, faces greater logistical hurdles in the modern digital economy.

Ultimately, the true scarcity of Bitcoin—enforced by cryptographic certainty and technological consensus—stands in stark contrast to the perceived scarcity of gold, which can fluctuate due to human discoveries and innovations. Bitcoin's fixed supply and deflationary nature position it as a unique asset in the modern financial landscape, offering a form of scarcity that is immune to the variables of human intervention, technological advancement, or the unknown frontiers of space.

Tokenization and Trust

In response to Bitcoin's growing prominence as a digital asset, some have proposed that gold can be tokenized—essentially creating digital tokens that represent physical gold stored in vaults—and used in a manner similar to Bitcoin. Tokenized gold allows for fractional ownership and easier transfer of value, potentially combining gold's historical role as a store of value with the efficiency and accessibility of digital assets. However, despite these theoretical advantages, the concept of tokenized gold introduces several practical challenges that significantly limit its appeal and efficacy compared to Bitcoin.

The first and most fundamental issue with tokenized gold is the need for a custodian. Because physical gold must be stored in vaults to back the digital tokens, users are required to trust a third party to accurately represent and safeguard the underlying gold reserves. This reliance on a custodian reintroduces one of the very problems that Bitcoin was designed to solve: the need for trust in intermediaries. Custodians can mismanage, over-leverage, or even defraud the system, as has occurred historically with gold reserves. Instances of gold reserves being misrepresented, either through fractional reserve practices or outright fraud, cast a shadow over the idea of tokenized gold being a reliable alternative to Bitcoin's trustless system.

This custodianship inherently carries risks that Bitcoin avoids through its decentralized architecture. In Bitcoin's system, there is no need to trust a central authority to hold or manage the asset. Instead, Bitcoin operates through a decentralized network where ownership is verified algorithmically by all participants in the blockchain. In contrast, tokenized gold reverts to a system dependent on human oversight, which is susceptible to corruption, error, and misrepresentation.

Additionally, the inherent challenge of verifying the physical gold that backs each token adds further complexity to a tokenized gold system. Unlike Bitcoin, where the supply is transparent, finite, and algorithmically controlled, gold is continually being mined and introduced into circulation. This presents significant verification issues for tokenized gold systems. As new gold enters the market, there must be processes in place to ensure that the physical gold backing the tokens is real, accurately accounted for, and free from duplication. This typically requires physical audits and centralized verification systems—processes that are both costly and vulnerable to manipulation or human error.

The complexity of auditing physical gold is another major disadvantage. In a tokenized system, auditing would have to be done regularly to confirm that the correct amount of gold is stored and linked to the corresponding tokens. Unlike Bitcoin, where every transaction and the total supply can be transparently verified by anyone at any time through the blockchain, tokenized gold requires trust in centralized audits conducted by third parties. These audits introduce delays, costs, and inefficiencies, further detracting from the promise of digital efficiency that tokenization attempts to deliver.

Moreover, tokenized gold still suffers from the same fundamental limitation as gold itself: it is not finite. While gold may be rare on Earth, its supply is not fixed, and new discoveries or advancements in mining technology can bring more gold into circulation. This poses a significant challenge for any tokenized system, as new gold must be continuously verified and incorporated into the existing system without compromising its integrity. As a result, tokenized gold remains vulnerable to supply inflation—an issue Bitcoin is explicitly designed to avoid.

In contrast, Bitcoin's supply is capped at 21 million, and this limit is enforced by the protocol itself. Bitcoin's decentralized nature and algorithmic verification ensure that no additional bitcoins can ever be created beyond this fixed limit, guaranteeing that Bitcoin cannot suffer from inflationary pressures due to an expanding supply. Every Bitcoin transaction is permanently recorded on a public blockchain, eliminating the need for trust in custodians, auditors, or centralized entities. This trustless, decentralized structure is a key reason why Bitcoin is viewed as a superior store of value in the digital age.

Finally, there is the issue of accessibility. Tokenized gold still exists within the physical world, meaning it remains subject to physical limitations, such as the need for secure storage, transportation, and handling. In times of crisis, access to the underlying gold reserves could be disrupted, whether by geopolitical factors, government intervention, or logistical challenges. Bitcoin, however, exists purely in the digital realm and can be accessed from anywhere in the world with an internet connection, providing unmatched liquidity and portability in comparison to any asset, including tokenized gold.

While the idea of tokenizing gold may offer a semblance of modernization to an ancient asset, it falls short of achieving the decentralization, transparency, and finite supply that Bitcoin inherently provides. The need for custodians, the complexity of verification, and the vulnerability to supply inflation make tokenized gold a fundamentally flawed attempt at replicating Bitcoin's unique attributes. As a result, tokenized gold remains a compromised solution that reintroduces many of the risks and inefficiencies that Bitcoin seeks to eliminate.

Network Anonymity and Decentralization

Finally, Bitcoin's decentralized and anonymous nature stands in stark contrast to any gold-backed system. The Bitcoin Network is maintained by thousands of independent nodes that verify transactions without the need for trust in a central authority or custodian. Transactions on the Bitcoin blockchain are pseudonymous, meaning that users can move value without revealing their personal information.

In a tokenized gold system, however, a digital network would still be required to verify and record transactions. This network would not be able to operate anonymously since it would involve third-party intermediaries and custodians. Users would need to trust these entities to accurately represent the gold they hold and ensure the integrity of transactions—an inherently centralized system. Moreover, the potential for corruption or fraud would always linger in a gold-backed digital system, which Bitcoin's decentralized, trustless architecture eliminates.

The New Era of Digital Sound Money

In the debate between Bitcoin and gold, it becomes clear that Bitcoin offers significant advantages as a store of value in the digital age. Its finite supply, low storage and transfer costs, and decentralized verification make it a more resilient and flexible asset compared to gold. While gold has a long history as a monetary standard, Bitcoin's unique properties position it as the future of sound money in a rapidly evolving financial landscape.

3

Bitcoin vs. The US Dollar

The US dollar has long held its place as the most powerful currency in the world, but its value is not immune to the forces of inflation and economic policies. While some may predict a doomsday scenario where the US dollar collapses and Bitcoin replaces it as the sole global monetary asset, the reality is likely more nuanced. This chapter will explore the comparative buying power of the US dollar versus Bitcoin, the history of the dollar as the global reserve currency, and how Bitcoin is positioned to become a major asset in the global economy.

The Declining Buying Power of the US Dollar

To understand the comparison between Bitcoin and the US dollar, it's crucial to recognize how much value the dollar has lost over the past few decades. Since the United States abandoned the gold standard in 1971, the dollar's purchasing power has steadily declined. For example, according to the U.S. Bureau of Labor Statistics, the dollar has lost approximately

85% of its value over the last 50 years. What you could buy for $1 in 1971 would now cost over $6.50. Inflation has eroded the dollar's buying power, and this trend shows no sign of reversing. In contrast, Bitcoin, which has a finite supply and an inflation-resistant design, has gained value since its inception, making it a strong hedge against inflation.

The Rise of the US Dollar as the Global Reserve Currency

The US dollar was once directly tied to gold, which provided the currency with intrinsic value. This era, known as the gold standard, meant that the value of the dollar was backed by physical gold reserves. However, in 1971, President Nixon removed the dollar from the gold standard, severing the link between the dollar and gold. This shift allowed the US to print money without requiring gold reserves to back it, which eventually led to inflation and a devaluation of the dollar over time.

Despite this, the US dollar remained the global reserve currency, largely due to a key geopolitical move in the 1970s. Henry Kissinger negotiated an agreement with Saudi Arabia to price oil exclusively in US dollars. This agreement solidified the dollar's position as the world's dominant currency for international trade, giving rise to the term "petrodollar." As oil is the lifeblood of the global economy, this move anchored the dollar's status for decades.

The Dollar's Declining Status and the Rise of Alternatives

Fast forward to today, and the dominance of the US dollar is facing unprecedented challenges. While the dollar remains the most powerful currency in the world, new economic powers are emerging, and the US's grip on global trade is weakening. One of the most significant threats to the dollar's hegemony is the spiraling national debt. As of October 2024, the US national debt has exceeded $35 trillion, and it's growing faster than ever before. The debt is currently increasing by approximately $1 trillion every three months, adding a staggering $9 trillion in just the past four years.

This rapid accumulation of debt signals a deeper problem—the sustainability of the US's financial model. The more the US government borrows, the less credible the dollar becomes as a store of value. The inflationary pressures caused by increasing the money supply to service this debt erode the dollar's purchasing power, making it less attractive both domestically and internationally. Moreover, the US is not alone. Many governments around the world are also adding massive amounts of debt, relying on fiat currencies that are not backed by anything tangible.

These developments are leading global players to question the long-term viability of the dollar as the world's reserve currency. Organizations like BRICS (Brazil, Russia, India, China, and South Africa) are actively seeking alternatives to the dollar for international trade. This shift is largely driven by the desire to reduce dependence on the US financial system, particularly in light of geopolitical tensions and the increasing volatility of the dollar.

Bitcoin, with its decentralized, borderless, and finite supply, presents itself as an attractive alternative. Unlike the dollar, Bitcoin is not tied to any one country's economy or policy decisions. Its fixed supply of 21 million coins ensures that it cannot be inflated or manipulated by any government. For countries looking to decouple from the US dollar's dominance, Bitcoin offers a potential solution—a store of value that is immune to political influence and economic instability.

Despite these challenges, the US dollar still reigns supreme—for now. Global assets, including real estate, commodities, and stocks valued at hundreds of trillions of dollars, are still priced in US dollars. The dollar's long-standing dominance, reinforced by the petrodollar system and the immense size of the US economy, continues to support its position as the world's reserve currency. However, this dominance is being eroded by the very policies that once propped it up. The continued printing of dollars to service ever-growing debt is unsustainable, and as inflation rises, so does the pressure on the dollar's global status.

The petrodollar system, which was born out of Henry Kissinger's negotiations to price oil exclusively in dollars, is fast becoming obsolete. As the world shifts toward alternative energy sources and countries seek to diversify their trade partners, the need for oil transactions to be priced exclusively in dollars is diminishing. BRICS nations and others are already looking at new frameworks for global trade, with some speculating that a cryptocurrency standard—perhaps led by Bitcoin—could replace the petrodollar in the years to come.

In this context, while the US dollar remains the most powerful currency, its future is increasingly uncertain. The spiraling national debt, inflationary pressures, and the rise of alternative currencies like Bitcoin are steadily undermining the dollar's long-held position. As countries and individuals alike look for more stable, transparent, and decentralized ways to store value, Bitcoin's appeal will only grow. It offers a way to escape the constant debasement of fiat currencies, providing a hedge against the inflation that is weakening not only the dollar but many other national currencies around the world.

The Bitcoin Comparison: A Hedge Against Dollar Debasement

Unlike the US dollar, Bitcoin's value has increased significantly since its creation. This difference stems from Bitcoin's built-in scarcity—only 21 million bitcoins will ever be mined. While the dollar has lost 85% of its value since leaving the gold standard, Bitcoin has gained tens of thousands of percent in value in the decade since its introduction. Its finite supply, decentralized nature, and global accessibility make it a powerful hedge against the continued debasement of the dollar.

For example, in the last decade, the value of Bitcoin has risen from less than a dollar to tens of thousands of dollars per Bitcoin. In contrast, the US dollar has consistently lost value due to inflation, which currently hovers around 3-4% annually.

This comparison illustrates the stark difference between a fiat currency that can be endlessly printed and a digital currency with a fixed supply.

A Likely Scenario: Dollar Inflation, Bitcoin Integration

While it's unlikely that the US dollar will collapse completely, the more likely scenario is that it will continue to inflate over time. The US government has no solid backing for the dollar apart from its historical dominance and the "good faith" of the US economy. On the other hand, Bitcoin's value is underpinned by its finite supply and the trust embedded in its immutable ledger.

This opens the door to a future where Bitcoin could potentially back the US dollar itself. Such a policy shift would allow the US economy to stabilize its currency using Bitcoin's fixed supply and decentralized trust mechanism. While this may seem unlikely today, it could become a necessary strategy to combat the ongoing debasement of the dollar.

However, there's no need to panic about a complete collapse of the US economy or the banking system. Instead, Bitcoin could save the ailing US economy by offering a digital reserve asset that backs national currencies. We could see a future where people continue to use dollars or local currencies for day-to-day transactions, but store their wealth in Bitcoin to hedge against inflation. Payment systems like Visa, Mastercard, and American Express may add a Bitcoin option, just as they do with various currencies, making it easier for consumers to use Bitcoin seamlessly alongside traditional payment methods.

One of Bitcoin's most powerful features is that it transcends borders, eliminating the need to convert from one currency to another in international trade. This can significantly reduce the cost and complexity of cross-border transactions, making global commerce more efficient. Whether for business-to-business transactions or individual consumers purchasing products via e-commerce, Bitcoin streamlines the process, reducing fees and transaction times. This advantage opens the door for small businesses to thrive in the global market, shrinking the barriers imposed by traditional financial systems and empowering entrepreneurs and consumers alike to engage in international trade without the friction of currency exchanges.

As e-commerce websites begin to accept Bitcoin payments, individuals will have more flexibility in how they spend their money, and businesses will benefit from reduced transaction costs and quicker payment settlements. In this way, Bitcoin isn't just a store of value—it's a tool that facilitates a more fluid and accessible global economy.

The Future of Bitcoin in the Global Economy

What's most likely is that Bitcoin will fully integrate into the global financial system as both an asset and a potential reserve currency. We might see Bitcoin used to back major transactions, including the buying and selling of commodities like oil. Bitcoin banks will emerge, making it easy for people and institutions to onramp and offramp from crypto into their local currencies. With platforms like Coinbase, Binance, and Kraken already enabling these transitions, the infrastructure is being built.

As institutional adoption of Bitcoin grows, large corporations and individual investors alike will use it to store value and make significant transactions. Bitcoin's flexibility, security, and global accessibility position it as the most versatile way to exchange goods, save wealth, and make large purchases.

As of October 2024, the versatility of Bitcoin is already evident in the multiple ways individuals and investors can engage with it. People can self-custody their own Bitcoin, use exchanges to trade and hold coins, invest in Bitcoin ETFs, or even include Bitcoin in retirement accounts like IRAs. Furthermore, companies are now holding Bitcoin as reserves on their balance sheets, a trend that reflects the growing confidence in Bitcoin as a long-term store of value. These varied options highlight the deepening integration of Bitcoin with traditional finance, a trend that will only continue as new financial products and services emerge.

In this sense, Bitcoin will not only compete with the US dollar but complement it. It will act as a global reserve asset, bringing stability to an increasingly volatile financial system while offering a safe haven for wealth. In a future where inflation continues to erode the value of fiat currencies, Bitcoin will become the most important store of value in the world.

Ultimately, there is no future for traditional finance without Bitcoin. Its growing presence in everything from corporate treasuries to personal investment portfolios signals that Bitcoin is no longer on the fringes of the financial world—it is becoming an integral part of it. As traditional finance continues to evolve, Bitcoin will be at the heart of this transformation, offering a bridge between old systems and the new, decentralized economy.

4

The Global Unbanked Crisis – Bitcoin as a Solution to Poverty

The Reality of the Unbanked

Despite living in an increasingly connected world, more than 1.4 billion people still lack access to basic financial services like bank accounts, loans, and safe places to store their money. These unbanked populations are primarily concentrated in developing countries, where financial infrastructure is either nonexistent or prohibitively expensive. For these individuals, the inability to participate in the formal financial system isn't just an inconvenience—it's a fundamental barrier to economic mobility.

Without access to secure savings, affordable loans, or the ability to invest in their futures, many unbanked individuals remain trapped in cycles of poverty. It's not a lack of effort or ingenuity that holds them back, but systemic exclusion from the global financial system. However, innovative solutions like Bitcoin and decentralized finance (DeFi) offer a path forward, bypassing traditional financial gatekeepers.

The Failure of Traditional Financial Systems to Serve the Poor

Traditional banking systems are designed for those with wealth and resources, often leaving the poor and unbanked out in the cold. To open a bank account, individuals typically need identification, a stable address, and a minimum balance—requirements that are unattainable for many living in poverty. Even in developed countries, millions remain underbanked, relying on expensive services like payday loans or check-cashing outlets, which charge exorbitant fees and further limit their ability to save and build wealth.

For many, the reality is harsh: despite working long hours, they have no safe place to store their earnings, making them vulnerable to theft or inflation in their local currency. Without savings or access to credit, they can't plan for emergencies, invest in their children's education, or start a business. These individuals are locked out of the global economy, forced to rely on predatory financial services that perpetuate financial instability.

Bitcoin and Decentralized Finance: A New Path to Financial Inclusion

Where traditional financial systems have failed, Bitcoin and decentralized finance (DeFi) provide a promising alternative. Built on blockchain technology, these platforms offer a wide range of financial services—such as loans, savings accounts, and insurance—without the need for banks or intermediaries. With just a smartphone and an internet connection, anyone can access the Bitcoin network or DeFi platforms, breaking down barriers that have long excluded millions from the financial system.

Bitcoin, in particular, is revolutionary for the unbanked. It eliminates the need for identification, a permanent address, or a minimum balance. Transactions are processed quickly, securely, and with minimal fees, giving unbanked populations access to financial tools that were previously out of reach. For the first time, people who have been excluded from the global economy can now participate in it using a decentralized system that is open and available to everyone.

DeFi complements Bitcoin by offering additional financial services like peer-to-peer lending, microfinance, and decentralized investment platforms, all without the need for traditional banks. Together, Bitcoin and DeFi are democratizing finance, fostering financial independence on a global scale.

Real-World Impact: Case Studies in Financial Stability

The real-world impact of Bitcoin as a lifeline for the unbanked is already evident in countries facing severe economic instability. In Venezuela, where hyperinflation has rendered the national currency nearly worthless, many citizens have turned to Bitcoin to preserve their wealth. By using Bitcoin, they can buy essential goods, make payments, and even trade on the global market, bypassing the failing traditional financial system.

Similarly, in Zimbabwe, Bitcoin has provided families with a way to maintain financial stability amid economic turmoil. In both cases, Bitcoin has proven to be the only reliable option for safeguarding personal wealth and participating in the global economy, where traditional currencies and banking systems have collapsed or are unreliable.

Bitcoin's Role in Reducing Financial Barriers

One of the most significant financial burdens for people in developing countries is the high cost of sending money across borders. Remittances—funds sent home by relatives working abroad—are often vital to supporting families, but traditional services like Western Union or MoneyGram charge fees as high as 10–15%. These costs can significantly reduce the amount of money that reaches families in need, often cutting into resources meant for food, education, or healthcare.

Bitcoin offers a solution to this problem by enabling low-cost, peer-to-peer transactions. Sending money across borders using Bitcoin incurs minimal fees, often a fraction of what traditional services charge. This means more of the money reaches its intended recipients, helping to alleviate the financial strain on families in developing nations.

Entrepreneurs and small businesses in these regions also benefit from Bitcoin's decentralized network. In areas where local currencies are unstable or financial services are scarce, Bitcoin enables business owners to accept payments from customers globally, bypassing high fees and complicated currency exchanges. Whether it's a street vendor in Indonesia or an artisan in Kenya, Bitcoin allows small businesses to connect with international customers, grow their business, and thrive in the global marketplace.

The Growing Wealth Gap: Traditional Banking's Role in Economic Inequality

While traditional banking systems have left millions unbanked, they have also contributed to a growing wealth gap in both developing and developed countries. As financial systems become more complex and reliant on high-cost services, the wealthy are able to leverage these systems to increase their wealth, while the poor are left with limited or expensive financial options. This wealth gap is exacerbated by rising costs of living, inflation, and stagnating wages, particularly among middle- and lower-income families.

Traditional banking favors those with wealth and access to resources. High-end financial services, including low-interest loans, wealth management, and investment opportunities, are available only to those who meet the stringent requirements of these institutions. Meanwhile, the underbanked and unbanked are forced to rely on costly alternatives like payday loans and check-cashing services, which only deepen their financial hardship. The result is a system that perpetuates inequality and accelerates the transfer of wealth into the hands of a few.

Bitcoin: Leveling the Financial Playing Field

Bitcoin offers a radically different approach. Unlike traditional banking systems, which are exclusive and often require a high level of wealth to access their best services, Bitcoin is open and available to anyone with a smartphone and an internet connection. There are no intermediaries, no gatekeepers, and no discriminatory practices. Bitcoin allows individuals to participate in a global financial system regardless of their wealth, geographic location, or access to traditional financial infrastructure.

For those in developing countries and for the unbanked, Bitcoin represents the first real opportunity to break free from the limitations imposed by traditional financial institutions. It enables anyone, anywhere, to save, invest, and transfer money without the high fees and restrictions of traditional banking. This inclusivity allows more people to accumulate and grow wealth, helping to reduce the economic disparities that have long plagued both developing and developed countries.

Bitcoin's decentralized nature also prevents the concentration of wealth in the hands of a few central authorities or financial elites. By removing intermediaries and making financial services accessible to all, Bitcoin has the potential to democratize wealth creation. It empowers individuals to control their own financial futures without relying on traditional systems that are skewed in favor of the wealthy.

The potential for Bitcoin to level the financial playing field is profound. As more people around the world gain access to this decentralized financial network, they will be able to participate in the global economy on equal terms. This shift represents not only a solution to the growing wealth gap but also an opportunity to create a more equitable and inclusive financial system for future generations.

Bitcoin as a Shield Against Corruption

In many developing countries, financial exclusion is exacerbated by corrupt governments and bureaucratic systems that prevent citizens from accessing basic financial services. Governments may freeze bank accounts, manipulate currency values, or impose arbitrary restrictions that keep people from accessing their own money. In these regions, even those with access to traditional financial systems may find that their wealth is not secure.

Bitcoin offers a solution by providing an immutable, decentralized ledger that no government can control. The blockchain ensures that every transaction is publicly recorded and cannot be tampered with, providing a level of transparency and security that is especially important in countries plagued by corruption. Bitcoin gives individuals the ability to protect their wealth from government overreach and inflation, offering financial stability in places where traditional currencies have failed.

Bitcoin as a Tool for Financial Sovereignty

Beyond offering financial inclusion, Bitcoin empowers individuals to take control of their own economic futures. In many developing countries, financial exclusion is compounded by unstable governments and poor economic policies. Citizens in these regions may find that their wealth can be threatened by currency manipulation or political interference. Bitcoin's decentralized and transparent nature provides individuals with a safeguard against these risks.

For millions around the world, Bitcoin represents more than just a technological innovation—it is a lifeline to financial sovereignty. It provides those who have been excluded from the traditional financial system the tools to finally achieve financial independence and participate in the global economy on their own terms. Bitcoin isn't just an alternative to traditional banking—it's the only viable path for the unbanked to secure their financial future and break free from cycles of poverty and exclusion.

5

The Halving Cycle and the Future of Mining: Sustaining Bitcoin's Decentralized Network

The Four-Year Halving Cycle and Bitcoin Mining

Bitcoin operates on a scheduled event known as the halving cycle, which occurs approximately every four years (or after every 210,000 blocks). During this event, the reward that miners receive for successfully adding a new block to the blockchain is cut in half. This systematic reduction is part of Bitcoin's deflationary design and ensures that the total supply of Bitcoin will never exceed 21 million. The halving mechanism was first activated in 2012, when the block reward dropped from 50 BTC to 25 BTC. After subsequent halvings, the reward fell to 12.5 BTC in 2016, then to 6.25 BTC in 2020, and as of 2024, it stands at 3.125 BTC per block.

This process not only limits the rate at which new Bitcoins are introduced into the system but also creates a sense of scarcity that influences Bitcoin's value. As the block rewards diminish, the supply of new Bitcoin becomes increasingly constrained, which is projected to continue until the year 2140 when the final Bitcoin is expected to be mined. After that point, no new Bitcoins will enter circulation, making the 21 million Bitcoin cap a permanent fixture of Bitcoin's economy.

The Role of Miners in the Bitcoin Network

Miners play a critical role in the Bitcoin network, not only in verifying transactions but also in maintaining the overall security of the blockchain. Through a process known as **proof-of-work**, miners solve complex cryptographic puzzles to validate and secure transactions, adding new blocks to the blockchain in exchange for rewards. This decentralized competition between miners ensures that no single entity can control or manipulate the network, maintaining the integrity of the system.

By verifying transactions, miners prevent double-spending, ensuring that Bitcoin is spent only once and that all transactions are legitimate. Additionally, this decentralized mining process contributes to the security and stability of the network, making it incredibly difficult for any individual or group to launch an attack. To tamper with Bitcoin's ledger, an attacker would need to control more than 50% of the network's mining power—a feat that becomes increasingly impractical as the network grows.

Currently, miners are incentivized through two primary means:

1. **Block Rewards**: This consists of newly minted Bitcoins, which miners receive upon successfully adding a block to the blockchain. However, with each halving event, this reward is reduced, decreasing the influx of new Bitcoins into circulation.
2. **Transaction Fees**: Every transaction sent across the network includes a fee paid by the sender. These fees incentivize miners to prioritize which transactions to include in the next block, especially when network activity increases, and block space becomes a valuable resource.

As the block rewards continue to diminish over time, transaction fees will become an increasingly significant part of the miners' compensation structure.

All Bitcoin Will Be Mined by 2140

Post-2140: What Happens After All Bitcoin is Mined?

One of the most commonly asked questions about Bitcoin's long-term viability is: What will incentivize miners to continue operating once all 21 million Bitcoins have been mined? After all, without the block rewards, which currently form a substantial portion of their income, how will miners remain profitable?

After 2140, when no more Bitcoins will be issued, the network will rely solely on transaction fees to incentivize miners. These fees will become the primary source of income for miners, and their importance will continue to grow as block rewards diminish after each halving event.

The theory is that as Bitcoin's supply becomes more limited and its adoption grows, its value will increase. This rise in value, combined with Bitcoin's growing utility as a medium of exchange and store of value, could lead to higher transaction fees in the future. As the global economy increasingly adopts Bitcoin, more users will generate more transactions, and the fees associated with those transactions could become substantial enough to provide sufficient incentives for miners to continue securing the network.

Moreover, Bitcoin's deflationary nature could attract more institutional players and large financial institutions who see Bitcoin as a hedge against inflation and an alternative to traditional assets like gold. As demand for Bitcoin increases in both speculative and practical uses (such as global remittances and cross-border transactions), miners may be able to rely on a steady stream of transactions with higher fees, even in the absence of block rewards.

Comparing Bitcoin's Mining Costs with Traditional Finance

A key comparison can be made between the operational costs of Bitcoin mining and those of the traditional banking system. Traditional financial institutions rely on a vast, highly centralized infrastructure to maintain operations, including physical bank branches, ATMs, massive data centers, payment processing systems, and a large workforce. The costs associated with maintaining this global infrastructure are immense, both in terms of financial resources and energy consumption.

Here are several major costs associated with traditional finance:

- **Real Estate**: Banks maintain costly physical locations, often in prime areas, to provide in-person services. These locations are not only expensive to lease or maintain but also require additional resources such as utilities, security, and maintenance staff.
- **Workforce**: The global banking system employs millions of people across various departments—ranging from customer service and tellers to IT support, compliance officers, and management. The salaries, benefits, and administrative costs associated with these employees are substantial.
- **Security**: Traditional financial institutions invest heavily in cybersecurity to prevent hacks and breaches, as well as physical security measures like vaults and safes to protect

assets. Additionally, banks allocate significant resources to fraud prevention, compliance with regulations, and insurance coverage to safeguard customers' money.
- **Payment Processing Networks**: Credit card companies and payment processing networks, such as Visa, MasterCard, and SWIFT, spend billions of dollars annually to maintain the infrastructure necessary for global payments. This includes server maintenance, data centers, and ensuring network reliability across multiple regions and time zones.

Bitcoin's mining operations, in comparison, are much more streamlined. The decentralized nature of the Bitcoin network eliminates the need for physical branches, customer service agents, and central authorities. Miners are essentially the backbone of the system, and their primary operational costs come from hardware (specialized machines known as ASIC miners) and electricity.

While Bitcoin mining does have an energy-intensive reputation due to the computational power required for proof-of-work, it is important to consider the broader context. Many miners are now turning to renewable energy sources, and innovative solutions like using surplus energy or waste heat are gaining popularity. This shift could significantly reduce the environmental and financial costs of mining over time.

Despite its energy demands, the costs of Bitcoin mining are minimal compared to the overall expenses of running the global financial system. As technological advancements make mining more energy-efficient, Bitcoin's decentralized network is poised to become even more cost-effective, further lowering barriers to entry and creating a financial system with far fewer overhead costs.

The Future: A More Efficient Global Financial System

As Bitcoin adoption increases, the decentralized network's efficiency becomes increasingly evident. Unlike traditional financial systems, which rely on centralized authorities and physical infrastructure, Bitcoin's network is purely digital and global. This shift from physical, location-dependent banking to a decentralized, digital financial infrastructure could result in significant cost savings and a more efficient system overall.

The costs of maintaining Bitcoin mining operations—while still substantial in the context of energy consumption—are expected to be dwarfed by the monumental expenses associated with the traditional global banking system. The decentralization of finance through Bitcoin could create a more streamlined, scalable, and efficient system that reduces reliance on costly infrastructure and intermediaries.

Moreover, as renewable energy sources become more widely adopted and integrated into Bitcoin mining, the environmental impact of the network could be further mitigated, enhancing Bitcoin's long-term viability. If miners can reduce their energy costs while maintaining the security and integrity of the network, Bitcoin could become an even more attractive alternative to the traditional financial system.

In the future, Bitcoin's decentralized network may lead to a more efficient global financial system—one that is not only more resilient and secure but also significantly less expensive to maintain. With fewer overhead costs, faster transactions, and increased transparency, Bitcoin has the potential to revolutionize the way the world conducts financial transactions.

Bitcoin's Place in the Evolving Financial Landscape

Bitcoin's halving cycle, miner incentives, and cost structures set it apart from traditional banking systems. While traditional financial institutions face significant overheads from real estate, personnel, and infrastructure, Bitcoin's decentralized, digital network operates with far fewer costs. As Bitcoin's value increases and adoption spreads, transaction fees will likely become the primary economic incentive for miners, ensuring that the network remains secure even after the last Bitcoin is mined.

In a world where efficiency, transparency, and reduced costs are increasingly critical, Bitcoin represents a major shift toward a decentralized global financial system. With fewer overheads and a potential for even greater energy efficiency, Bitcoin may become the foundation of a future financial network—one that is more inclusive, efficient, and secure.

6

Bitcoin as Conserved Monetary Energy

Understanding Conserved Monetary Energy

Bitcoin advocate and entrepreneur Michael Saylor has popularized the idea of Bitcoin as "conserved monetary energy." At its core, this concept suggests that Bitcoin enables individuals and institutions to store financial energy—representing the value created through work, trade, and investment—in a secure, efficient, and lasting way. This is particularly significant when compared to traditional forms of money, which are subject to erosion over time due to inflation, currency devaluation, or government intervention.

In the same way that humanity has learned to harness physical energy through advancements in technology—such as the steam engine or renewable energy—Bitcoin offers a revolutionary method of conserving and protecting monetary value in the digital age. Unlike fiat currencies, which can be printed at will and lose value through inflation, Bitcoin's fixed supply of 21 million coins creates an economic structure where value is preserved rather than diminished. By eliminating the risks of monetary inflation, Bitcoin mirrors the principles of conservation found in efficient energy systems: limited resources, maximized output, and minimal waste.

Traditional currencies, held in banks or physical assets like gold, can degrade in value or be seized by governments. Bitcoin addresses this risk by offering a decentralized, immutable network where financial energy can be stored without reliance on a central authority. In this context, Bitcoin acts as a battery for monetary energy, storing value securely and allowing it to be transferred globally with minimal friction.

The Bitcoin Network Monetizes Energy

How Bitcoin Mirrors Technological Advances in Energy Conservation

Throughout history, humanity has innovated ways to conserve and use physical energy more effectively. The invention of the steam engine, internal combustion engine, and advancements in renewable energy technology allowed industries like manufacturing, transportation, and agriculture to do more with less. These innovations reduced energy waste, maximized labor output, and transformed the global economy by making processes more efficient.

Bitcoin applies this same principle of efficiency to the financial system. In traditional finance, transferring money internationally or making investments often involves high costs, delays, and numerous intermediaries, all of which siphon off value. These inefficiencies are akin to energy leakage in physical systems—waste that Bitcoin seeks to eliminate.

In contrast to traditional banking, Bitcoin's decentralized system eliminates the need for intermediaries such as banks, clearinghouses, and payment processors. Transactions are conducted directly between parties, without the friction of fees, delays, or regulatory hurdles. This process reduces the so-called "monetary energy leakage" that occurs in the traditional financial system, conserving more of the value generated by individuals and businesses.

For example, transferring funds through traditional financial networks often involves hidden fees for currency conversion, processing delays, and time-consuming regulatory approvals.

With Bitcoin, these inefficiencies disappear. Payments are made directly, quickly, and at a lower cost. The financial value that might have been lost through banking fees or inflated transaction costs is preserved, aligning with the idea of conserving energy and reducing waste.

Bitcoin's Role in Reducing Monetary Friction

Monetary friction refers to the various obstacles that hinder the movement of value in the traditional financial system. These obstacles take the form of credit card fees, wire transfer delays, currency exchange costs, and administrative barriers. For businesses and individuals alike, these frictions represent a loss of financial energy—value that is consumed by the intermediaries of the global banking system.

Bitcoin reduces this friction by offering a decentralized, borderless platform for transferring value. Unlike traditional banks, which are constrained by national borders, regulatory frameworks, and operating hours, Bitcoin operates globally and 24/7, allowing value to be transferred instantly and with minimal cost. This efficiency is particularly valuable in industries that rely on global trade, where speed and cost-effectiveness are crucial.

For example, a small business owner who wants to sell goods internationally would face multiple financial frictions using the traditional banking system. They would need to convert currencies, pay wire transfer fees, and wait for several days for payments to clear. Bitcoin simplifies this process by allowing for near-instantaneous payments without the need for third-party verification or currency conversion. The result is faster, cheaper, and more efficient transactions that conserve more of the monetary energy involved in the transaction.

In this sense, Bitcoin is akin to the technological innovations that revolutionized transportation, such as the internal combustion engine, which drastically reduced the friction of moving goods across distances. Just as that technology made physical movement more efficient, Bitcoin is making the movement of value across borders more frictionless and conserving the energy—monetary or otherwise—that might have been lost along the way.

Traditional Banking vs. Bitcoin's Energy Efficiency

Bitcoin is often criticized for its energy consumption, particularly in relation to the energy-intensive process of mining, which uses computational power to secure the network. However, this criticism overlooks the significant energy consumption of the traditional banking system, which also requires vast resources to maintain its infrastructure.

The traditional banking system relies on an extensive network of physical branches, data centers, and a global workforce. Each financial institution incurs substantial energy costs, from powering office buildings and ATMs to operating data centers that handle millions of transactions daily. Additionally, the global payment systems that underpin modern finance, such as Visa, MasterCard, and SWIFT, also demand enormous amounts of energy to ensure the smooth processing of transactions across borders.

Banks not only require physical space and manpower but also a significant energy investment in cybersecurity, fraud prevention, and customer support. Maintaining these operations involves not just financial costs but also an environmental footprint.

The Greenest Energy on Earth

In contrast, Bitcoin's energy usage is focused solely on securing the network and validating transactions. While Bitcoin's **Proof of Work** consensus mechanism does require substantial energy, it's important to consider that much of this energy is increasingly sourced from renewable resources. Bitcoin miners, particularly those in regions with abundant renewable energy, such as hydroelectric power or geothermal energy, have turned to these alternatives to reduce costs and improve sustainability.

Bitcoin's energy efficiency, when compared to the global banking system, presents a striking contrast. While traditional banks require physical infrastructure, personnel, and complex layers of intermediaries, Bitcoin operates in a purely digital space with minimal human intervention. The elimination of physical branches, central authorities, and third-party processors means that Bitcoin's energy is spent exclusively on securing the network, rather than maintaining the elaborate infrastructure of traditional banks.

As renewable energy sources become more widespread, Bitcoin's mining operations are expected to shift further toward sustainability. This transition could make Bitcoin an even greener alternative to traditional banking, whose reliance on fossil fuels and other energy-intensive processes continues to be a concern in the fight against climate change.

A Future with More Efficient Financial Energy

As the world increasingly embraces digital finance, Bitcoin offers a glimpse of a future in which the energy used for financial transactions is significantly more efficient. While the traditional banking system consumes massive amounts of energy to power physical infrastructure and maintain global payment networks, Bitcoin's decentralized approach bypasses these limitations, operating entirely in the digital realm.

In the long term, Bitcoin's energy consumption may become even more efficient, particularly as renewable energy adoption grows and technological advancements improve mining efficiency. Meanwhile, the legacy financial system may continue to face significant challenges as it seeks to reduce its environmental impact while maintaining the complex infrastructure required to facilitate global commerce.

By reducing friction, eliminating intermediaries, and securing monetary value in a decentralized and transparent way, Bitcoin represents a more energy-efficient future for finance. It conserves monetary energy by reducing the waste and inefficiency inherent in traditional financial systems, offering a streamlined alternative that aligns with the broader global shift toward sustainability and technological innovation.

A Greener Future for Global Finance

While Bitcoin's energy consumption is often criticized, a deeper look reveals that it may offer a more sustainable and efficient financial model compared to traditional banking. The inefficiencies of the legacy banking system—driven by its reliance on physical infrastructure, manpower, and intermediaries—are significant contributors to energy waste. In contrast, Bitcoin's decentralized network, powered increasingly by renewable energy, presents a compelling alternative for a future where financial transactions are faster, less costly, and more environmentally friendly.

As Bitcoin continues to evolve, it will likely play an important role in creating a more energy-efficient global financial system, aligning with advancements in renewable energy and digital infrastructure. The idea of "conserved monetary energy" demonstrates how Bitcoin is more than just a cryptocurrency—it is a fundamental shift in how we store, move, and protect value in an increasingly digital and energy-conscious world.

7

Historical Examples of Energy Conservation Driving Prosperity

Agriculture: From Hand Labor to Mechanized Farming

The agricultural sector provides one of the clearest examples of how humanity has learned to conserve energy and increase prosperity. In the early days of civilization, agriculture was entirely dependent on human and animal labor. Farmers had to till the land, plant seeds, and harvest crops by hand, a labor-intensive process that consumed a massive amount of human energy while yielding relatively low output. As populations grew, it became increasingly clear that this system was unsustainable.

The **Industrial Revolution** changed everything. The introduction of mechanized tools—like the tractor, irrigation systems, and automated harvesters—drastically reduced the amount of human energy required to farm the land. **Tractors** replaced manual plowing, allowing farmers to cultivate larger areas in less time. **Irrigation systems** conserved water, ensuring crops could grow in dry regions, and **fertilizers** helped increase crop yields. These technological innovations were all forms of energy conservation—allowing humans to achieve more with less effort.

Today, we've moved even further. **Precision agriculture** utilizes drones, sensors, and data analytics to monitor soil conditions, determine the exact needs of crops, and apply water and nutrients only where necessary, reducing waste. The global food distribution system now operates on an enormous scale—food is grown in one part of the world, processed and packaged in another, and distributed to stores across continents.

Manufacturing: The Rise of Automation

The **manufacturing sector** has undergone a similar revolution. In the pre-industrial world, artisans handcrafted goods in small quantities. Each item was painstakingly made by hand, requiring significant labor and skill. This method was highly inefficient, limiting the ability to produce goods at scale and restricting access to products for the average person.

The advent of the **Industrial Revolution** introduced **mass production**, a method that conserved human energy by utilizing machinery. The assembly line, pioneered by **Henry Ford**, transformed the way goods were produced. Machines performed repetitive tasks, reducing human effort and allowing factories to produce vast quantities of items quickly and efficiently.

Transportation: The Internal Combustion Engine and Global Supply Chains

Transportation is another industry that has undergone a revolution in energy conservation. In ancient times, the primary method of moving people and goods was **human or animal power**. People walked, used horses or donkeys, or relied on simple wooden carts. This was slow, inefficient, and limited the distance that goods could be transported.

The invention of the **internal combustion engine** transformed transportation. **Cars, trucks, airplanes, and ships** dramatically increased the speed and scale of movement, allowing goods to be moved quickly across vast distances. This conserved human energy that was once spent on manual transport, opening new markets for trade and reshaping the global economy.

Energy: The Shift from Fossil Fuels to Renewables

The **energy sector** itself has gone through dramatic transformations in terms of conservation. In the earliest days of industrialization, humans relied heavily on **coal** and **wood** as energy sources. These fuels were abundant but inefficient and highly polluting. The discovery of **oil** and **natural gas** ushered in a new era of energy consumption, powering the growth of the industrialized world and enabling modern infrastructure, transportation, and technology.

However, as the environmental costs of fossil fuels became clear, the world began shifting toward **renewable energy sources** like wind, solar, and hydroelectric power. These sources not only conserve natural resources but also reduce the pollution and carbon emissions associated with traditional fossil fuels.

Communications: The Internet Revolution

The communications sector provides yet another compelling example of energy conservation driving human progress. In the past, communication over long distances was slow and labor-intensive. People relied on couriers or the postal service to deliver messages, which could take days, weeks, or even months to reach their destination.

The invention of the **telegraph** in the 19th century, followed by the **telephone** in the early 20th century, revolutionized communication by allowing people to exchange information instantly across vast distances. However, these technologies still required significant physical infrastructure, such as telephone lines and switching stations.

The rise of the **internet** in the late 20th century took communication to a new level of efficiency. Today, we can send messages, make video calls, and share vast amounts of data across the globe in a matter of seconds—all with minimal energy consumption compared to earlier methods. The internet allows for the global transmission of ideas, collaboration, and commerce, shrinking the world into a connected digital network.

Bitcoin's Parallels with Energy Conservation

Just as society has progressed by conserving physical energy, Bitcoin represents a similar advancement in how we conserve and store financial value. Like the steam engine or the internal combustion engine, Bitcoin maximizes efficiency by reducing waste—this time in the form of monetary friction. It allows value to move faster, cheaper, and more securely than ever before.

By understanding how technological innovations in energy conservation have driven prosperity, it becomes clear that Bitcoin has the potential to do the same for the global financial system. It offers a more efficient way to store and transfer value, just as modern energy systems offer a more efficient way to power our world.

8

Bitcoin, Transparency, and the Global Financial System

The Problem with Traditional Financial Transparency

One of the defining differences between Bitcoin and traditional finance is transparency—or rather, the lack of it in the current financial system. In traditional finance, many processes and transactions are concealed from public view, creating an environment where corruption, fraud, and misuse thrive. Offshore banking, secret accounts, and complex financial instruments allow powerful individuals and organizations to operate outside the law, evade taxes, and fund illicit activities.

This lack of transparency was a key factor in the 2008 financial crisis, where hidden financial practices, such as mortgage-backed securities and derivatives trading, pushed the global economy to the brink of collapse. While governments stepped in to rescue financial institutions, the true cost fell on ordinary citizens, many of whom lost their homes, jobs, and savings. The obscure nature of traditional finance left people powerless, with little insight or recourse, and highlighted the inherent dangers of secrecy in the financial system.

Without transparency, accountability in finance is nearly impossible. Institutions can obscure their activities, making it difficult to track how money is spent, invested, or even manipulated. This lack of oversight not only destabilizes economies but also undermines public trust in financial and governmental institutions.

Traditional Finance and Hidden Corruption

Bitcoin's Transparent Blockchain Solution

Bitcoin offers a revolutionary alternative to this hidden system through its transparent and decentralized ledger, the blockchain. Every transaction on Bitcoin's network is recorded publicly and immutably, creating a system where no transaction can be hidden, altered, or erased. This open ledger means that anyone—whether an individual, a business, or a government—

can independently verify any transaction. Bitcoin's blockchain eliminates the need for trust in third parties, as the system itself provides the proof of every financial exchange.

What sets Bitcoin apart is that, while the blockchain is completely transparent, individual transactions remain pseudonymous. This means that although the financial movements are visible for anyone to see, the identities of the parties involved are protected. This balance between privacy and transparency allows for accountability without compromising individual privacy—something neither traditional finance nor centralized digital payment systems have fully achieved.

The transparency of the blockchain fundamentally alters how trust operates in the financial world. With Bitcoin, there is no need to rely on intermediaries, such as banks or government institutions, to verify the legitimacy of transactions. Instead, the network itself serves as an unbiased and incorruptible source of truth, making it virtually impossible for individuals or institutions to engage in fraudulent or manipulative activities without being detected.

Real-World Applications of Bitcoin Transparency

The transparency of Bitcoin's blockchain is already being utilized to create more accountable financial systems. A prime example is **El Salvador**, the first nation to adopt Bitcoin as legal tender. The country has implemented blockchain-based measures to ensure government spending is publicly verifiable, setting a precedent for how Bitcoin can force transparency at a governmental level. Citizens can track how public funds are allocated and ensure that government spending is legitimate—a level of transparency never before seen in the realm of national finance.

In regions where corruption is rampant, Bitcoin's transparency could act as a powerful tool to restore public trust. By enabling citizens to monitor how their taxes are used, it offers a way to hold governments accountable and reduce the misuse of public funds. This shift toward transparent governance has the potential to radically alter the dynamics of how financial power is wielded, especially in developing countries plagued by institutional corruption.

Global Implications: From Financial Trust to Peace

The implications of financial transparency extend beyond simply holding institutions accountable. On a global scale, opaque financial systems have historically fueled conflict, corruption, and instability. Shadowy financial flows through tax havens, offshore accounts, and secretive banking networks have enabled dictatorships to thrive, wars to be funded, and governments to be toppled, all while leaving ordinary citizens to pay the price.

In contrast, Bitcoin's transparency offers a path toward greater financial accountability, one that could help foster global stability and peace. If governments and corporations were required to use Bitcoin or adopt a Bitcoin standard, they would no longer be able to hide their financial dealings. The blockchain's public ledger would expose illicit activities and hold powerful actors accountable, reducing opportunities for corruption and exploitation.

A government running on Bitcoin would find it far more difficult to print money indiscriminately or covertly fund wars. Without the ability to inflate their currency at will, governments would be forced to live within their means and manage their finances responsibly. They would need to focus on spending money for the benefit of their citizens rather than treating their resources like an endless pool. By preventing financial mismanagement and secrecy, Bitcoin could reduce the ability of states to fund conflict and perpetuate violence.

A New Era of Accountability

Bitcoin's transparency could also act as a force for peace by addressing the root causes of conflict. In many war-torn or economically unstable regions, citizens suffer under corrupt regimes that manipulate local currencies, seize assets, and use financial control as a tool of oppression. Bitcoin offers these citizens an escape—a decentralized, transparent system where they can store and protect their wealth, free from government interference or inflationary policies.

When people are empowered with financial sovereignty, the dynamics of power begin to shift. Governments that rely on financial control to oppress their populations would face increasing resistance as citizens adopt Bitcoin and exit the traditional systems of control. Moreover, as more nations and regions adopt Bitcoin and incorporate its principles of transparency, we could see a new global standard for financial governance. With fewer opportunities for covert operations and illicit funding, the likelihood of large-scale conflicts driven by hidden agendas would diminish.

The transparency enforced by Bitcoin could serve as a catalyst for a more peaceful world. Governments would no longer be able to secretly allocate resources to military campaigns or covert operations to destabilize other nations. This financial openness would make it far more difficult to initiate or sustain conflicts without public scrutiny and accountability.

Bitcoin's Potential as a Catalyst for Global Peace

The potential for Bitcoin to reshape global power dynamics cannot be overstated. By enforcing financial accountability and transparency, Bitcoin challenges the very foundations of how governments and institutions operate. No longer can powerful entities hide behind the veil of secrecy to manipulate economies, exploit resources, or fund conflicts. With Bitcoin, every financial action is visible and verifiable on the blockchain, making it far more difficult to engage in covert or corrupt activities.

As Bitcoin adoption grows, we could witness a profound shift toward global financial accountability. Governments would be forced to prioritize responsible spending, investing in their citizens and infrastructure rather than engaging in wasteful or harmful practices. Without the ability to print money to cover deficits or launch wars, governments would need to manage their resources efficiently and work within their means. This newfound accountability could promote a more stable and peaceful world, as the financial motivations behind many conflicts would be exposed and curtailed.

Bitcoin's decentralized, transparent system offers a new form of financial governance—one where secrecy, corruption, and financial mismanagement are no longer tolerated. As more people and institutions adopt Bitcoin, the pressure on traditional systems to become more transparent and accountable will only increase. In this way, Bitcoin not only revolutionizes finance but also holds the potential to transform global governance and peace.

Fostering Global Collaboration and the Creative Economy

Beyond financial transactions, Bitcoin is also playing a role in fostering a new era of global collaboration and creativity. Its decentralized, borderless nature transcends geographical limitations, allowing individuals from different parts of the world to collaborate and innovate in ways that were previously impossible. This has given rise to the "creative economy," where artists, developers, and creators can monetize their work directly without needing intermediaries like publishers or distributors.

For example, digital artists and content creators can now sell their work directly to a global audience using Bitcoin. Payments are instant, secure, and free from the delays and fees that often come with traditional payment systems. This opens up new markets and opportunities for creative professionals, particularly those who may have been marginalized by the centralized systems of the past.

The ability to exchange value instantly and globally has also made international collaborations much more efficient. Developers in Africa, Asia, and South America can work together on projects without the complications of banking arrangements or high transfer fees. Bitcoin, in this sense, serves as the backbone for a global network of innovation, connecting people, ideas, and resources across borders.

BITCOIN UTOPIA:

A Transparent Path Forward

Bitcoin represents more than just a new form of money—it offers a vision of a more transparent, accountable, and peaceful world. By removing the ability of governments to secretly manipulate currencies, fund wars, or engage in covert activities, Bitcoin introduces a new standard of financial transparency that could lead to greater global stability. With fewer opportunities for corruption and hidden agendas, the likelihood of conflict diminishes, while citizens gain more control over their financial futures.

As we move toward a future where transparency is not just an option but a requirement, Bitcoin has the potential to be a powerful force for peace. By enforcing accountability on a global scale, Bitcoin could help create a world where financial secrecy no longer fuels conflict, and governments are held to the highest standards of transparency and responsibility.

9

Conclusion – A Future Powered by Bitcoin

Bitcoin's Role in Shaping the Future of Finance

Bitcoin is not just a technological breakthrough—it represents a fundamental shift in how we understand financial systems, governance, and global economic fairness. As the financial landscape evolves, Bitcoin stands at the forefront, offering a revolutionary approach to money, value, and financial inclusion. By providing access to financial services for billions of unbanked individuals, removing costly intermediaries, and offering a transparent, secure system for storing and transferring value, Bitcoin is reshaping the future of finance.

For Bitcoin enthusiasts, the vision extends far beyond an alternative currency. Bitcoin is the foundation of a decentralized, transparent global financial system where everyone, regardless of location or wealth, can participate on equal footing. It's not just a store of value—it becomes the bedrock for a new economic order that touches every aspect of life, enabling individuals worldwide to take control of their financial destiny.

Don't Miss Out on this Global Revolution

Bitcoin Utopia: A Decentralized Global Network

Bitcoiners see a future where Bitcoin is the backbone of global trade, finance, and governance, enabling a system free from corruption, inefficiency, and centralized control. This "Bitcoin Utopia" envisions a world where Bitcoin serves as a universal standard for value, supporting decentralized finance (DeFi), tokenized assets, and innovative financial solutions. In this decentralized ecosystem, participation is open to all, offering equal access to the global economy.

A key element of this future is the ability to leverage Bitcoin as a financial asset. As Bitcoin's value grows, individuals will be able to borrow against their holdings, much like traditional assets such as real estate or stocks. This unlocks liquidity without the need to sell Bitcoin, empowering people worldwide—especially those in regions with unreliable banking systems or volatile currencies—to access loans, start businesses, or invest in their futures.

Bitcoin as a Borrowing Asset

As Bitcoin's value and stability grow, individuals will be able to leverage their Bitcoin holdings, much like traditional assets such as real estate or stocks are used as collateral today. In this system, Bitcoiners can access loans without needing to sell their Bitcoin, opening the door to liquidity without sacrificing long-term wealth.

Financial institutions and decentralized platforms will offer loans based on the value of an individual's Bitcoin holdings, providing a cost-effective way to unlock value. Since Bitcoin is recognized as a stable and highly valuable asset, interest rates on these loans would be minimal. This feature offers financial freedom to people worldwide, particularly those in regions with unreliable banking systems or volatile currencies. For instance, a person in a developing country could borrow against their Bitcoin holdings to start a business, invest in education, or improve their living conditions.

In wealthier nations, Bitcoin-backed loans would serve as a hedge against inflation or economic downturns, allowing individuals to access capital without liquidating assets during uncertain times. This mechanism empowers people across the globe to participate in the economy, unlock new opportunities, and improve their financial stability.

A Global Network for Everyone

Bitcoin's decentralized nature offers the potential for universal participation. Anyone, anywhere, could contribute to the network, whether by running nodes, participating in mining, or offering computational resources to help maintain and secure the blockchain. As technology evolves, this participation will become more accessible, moving beyond large industrial operations to smaller, decentralized efforts.

For example, individuals could contribute surplus renewable energy, like solar power, to Bitcoin mining operations and earn small rewards. In colder climates, Bitcoin mining rigs might be used to generate heat while also validating transactions, making energy consumption both productive and financially rewarding. This model would allow people across the world—whether in wealthy nations or developing countries—to earn Bitcoin by contributing to the network's security and functionality, creating a self-sustaining ecosystem.

Bitcoin's decentralized financial system creates a level playing field where wealth generation is not restricted by traditional barriers. Financial inclusion becomes more than just access to money; it empowers individuals to actively contribute to the global economy, fostering a truly democratic system of participation and wealth creation.

Earning Through Engagement

As automation and artificial intelligence continue to replace traditional jobs, there is growing concern about how society will adapt to widespread employment changes. Bitcoin could offer a unique solution through universal participation in the network, where rewards are distributed not as passive income but as a result of active engagement with the system.

In this future, Bitcoin's decentralized infrastructure would allow individuals to earn small amounts of Bitcoin through everyday participation, whether by contributing computational power, energy resources, or innovative solutions that optimize the network. These micro-contributions could add up over time, resulting in a steady stream of rewards from the Bitcoin network. As Bitcoin's value continues to grow, even small payouts could accumulate into meaningful financial resources, potentially enough to support basic living expenses for people around the world.

Instead of relying on a central government to distribute wealth, the Bitcoin network itself—through its self-regulating nature—would provide financial incentives for participation. In this way, the rewards people receive would be tied to their contribution to maintaining and improving the network, creating a meritocratic system where everyone has the opportunity to benefit.

Innovations in AI could lead to the development of algorithms that optimize the Bitcoin network's efficiency, and individuals who create or maintain these technologies might receive compensation in the form of Bitcoin. Additionally, those who contribute to securing the network by validating transactions, running nodes, or participating in decentralized energy-sharing systems would also be rewarded. As more people find ways to contribute, the financial rewards would be distributed across a broader population, allowing even those who lack access to traditional employment opportunities to earn a living.

Here are a few examples of how people might engage with the Bitcoin network, demonstrating the global adaptability and resourcefulness of individuals in this new decentralized economy:

1. **Solar-Powered Mining in Rural Communities**
   In many developing countries, access to electricity is unreliable, but solar energy is abundant. Imagine a rural village in West Africa where individuals set up small-scale, solar-powered Bitcoin mining operations. These setups, powered by off-grid solar panels, allow communities to contribute computational power to the Bitcoin network. Over time, these villages could earn Bitcoin through their mining efforts, and even small amounts of Bitcoin could accumulate into significant resources. The Bitcoin

earned could be used to fund essential local projects, such as building schools, improving water infrastructure, or providing healthcare.

2. **Microtasks and Digital Services for Bitcoin Payments**
   In regions where traditional employment is scarce, individuals are already turning to digital platforms that pay in Bitcoin. For example, in Venezuela, young adults could earn Bitcoin by completing microtasks online, such as data labeling for AI algorithms or providing freelance services like graphic design and website development. By working through platforms that compensate in Bitcoin, these individuals bypass the hyperinflation of their local currency, preserving their earnings in a more stable asset. Over time, these small transactions could accumulate and provide a reliable source of income in an otherwise unstable economy.

3. **Decentralized Energy-Sharing Networks**
   In remote areas of India, where electricity access is still a challenge, communities might engage in decentralized energy-sharing systems. Villages could install wind turbines or hydropower generators to produce electricity. Rather than letting excess energy go to waste, these communities could use the surplus power to run Bitcoin mining machines. By contributing renewable energy to power the network, the community would earn Bitcoin in return. This new form of economic participation would create an incentive for local energy production while providing a steady source of income that could support long-term development in these rural regions.

4. **Waste-to-Wealth: Frying Oil-Powered Bitcoin Mining**
   In Southeast Asia, a resourceful individual might find an

innovative way to turn waste into income. Equipped with a scooter, this entrepreneur collects used frying oil from local food vendors and restaurants, filters it at home, and uses it to fuel a small generator. The generator, in turn, powers an ASIC Bitcoin mining machine, allowing the individual to mine Bitcoin. What was once a discarded material now becomes a valuable resource, contributing to the Bitcoin network and generating income. This example showcases the ingenuity and creativity that Bitcoin's decentralized nature encourages, turning what would otherwise be waste into wealth.

5. **Cross Border and Global Remittances**
   In the Philippines, families rely heavily on remittances from relatives working abroad. With Bitcoin, sending remittances becomes faster and cheaper, bypassing traditional remittance services that often charge exorbitant fees. A family in Manila might receive Bitcoin directly from a relative in the United States, eliminating the need for middlemen like Western Union. Not only does this provide faster access to funds, but it also helps the family store value in a more stable currency. Over time, Bitcoin could become a preferred method for remittances in many developing countries, providing families with more financial freedom and security.

These examples illustrate just a few of the ways people around the world might creatively engage with and benefit from the Bitcoin network. The decentralized nature of Bitcoin opens up new economic opportunities that are not reliant on existing infrastructure or central authorities. Instead, individuals can participate directly, using whatever resources they have at their disposal—whether it's solar energy, digital services, or even used frying oil.

The idea of everyone on the planet participating in the Bitcoin network and receiving rewards turns the concept of wealth creation on its head. Beyond traditional sources of support like fixed incomes or social programs, the Bitcoin network offers individuals new opportunities to supplement their income through innovation, energy contribution, or computational power, offering new ways to create and build wealth! Over time, this model could help mitigate the economic inequality caused by automation and globalization, providing a decentralized, borderless solution to the financial challenges of the 21st century.

In this future, the Bitcoin network would not only function as a global financial infrastructure but also as a platform for economic empowerment. The rewards distributed across the network could serve as a lifeline for individuals displaced by automation, providing a financial safety net without relying on traditional employment. This system would be built on active engagement, rewarding those who participate in and contribute to the network's ongoing development and security.

Government and Corporate Transparency on the Blockchain

The transparency provided by Bitcoin's blockchain is another key element of this vision. In a world where Bitcoin is the standard, governments, corporations, and individuals alike would have their financial transactions recorded on the blockchain for public scrutiny. This level of transparency would eliminate corruption and hold powerful entities accountable. Governments and corporations could no longer operate in secrecy, as every financial action would be visible and verifiable by anyone with access to the blockchain.

This system of transparency would not only prevent misuse of public funds but also create a fairer and more just society. Citizens would be able to track how governments allocate resources and ensure that public spending benefits the greater good. The days of opaque financial dealings would be over, replaced by a system of accountability and integrity.

Politicians Held Accountable by a Transparent Financial System

In this Bitcoin-powered world, the role of politicians would fundamentally shift. Today, many politicians make grand promises, often backed by hidden government spending, without clear mechanisms for accountability. In a world governed by Bitcoin's transparency, such financial mismanagement would be exposed in real-time.

The decentralized nature of Bitcoin's blockchain would ensure that every allocation of government resources is recorded immutably. Politicians would no longer have the ability to print money or mismanage funds without public scrutiny. Instead, they would be constrained by transparent budgets and held accountable by the citizens they serve. This would foster a healthier relationship between governments and the public, where leaders are judged by their ability to manage resources effectively and fairly.

Opening Access to Global Investment Through Tokenized Assets

In the future envisioned by Bitcoin proponents, the tokenization of assets on the blockchain will revolutionize how people invest, making it possible for anyone—regardless of their financial situation—to participate in global investment opportunities. Assets that were once the exclusive domain of the wealthy, such as masterpieces by Van Gogh, high-end real estate, luxury goods, or even commercial ventures like golf courses, can be fractionally owned and traded by people around the world.

Tokenized assets allow these previously inaccessible investments to be broken down into smaller, more affordable units, enabling participation by individuals who would never have had the opportunity in today's traditional financial system. This is especially significant for underprivileged populations, who, for the first time, could invest in assets that were once out of reach due to geographical or monetary barriers.

For example, a person living in a developing nation could own a fractional share of a high-value real estate property in New York or a piece of a rare work of art stored in a gallery on the other side of the world. Through tokenization, anyone with access to the Bitcoin network and blockchain technology could buy, sell, or trade portions of these assets in a secure, transparent marketplace.

This shift democratizes wealth-building by making global assets available to all, creating a financial environment where people from all walks of life can diversify their portfolios, participate in global markets, and generate wealth. The barriers to entry—such as high costs, lack of access, or financial gatekeeping—are erased. Tokenization ensures that markets remain open, fair, and accessible, providing a true equal opportunity for wealth generation.

As more assets are tokenized on the blockchain, this trend will transform the very nature of investment. Instead of relying on traditional brokers, banks, or intermediaries to facilitate large transactions, individuals can participate directly in global markets, often with minimal fees and full transparency. This model of fractional ownership and blockchain-based trading will not only unlock new opportunities for financial growth but also help stabilize asset values through open and decentralized markets.

In this future, Bitcoin's role as the global standard of value, combined with the tokenization of assets, will help create a more inclusive and equitable financial system. Everyone, regardless of their initial wealth or financial status, will have the chance to invest in and own pieces of the world's most valuable assets, leveling the playing field for generations to come.

The Blockchain is Immutable

Bitcoin and Generational Wealth

While Bitcoin's value continues to rise, there remains a unique window of opportunity for individuals to invest and secure financial stability not only for themselves but also for their descendants. Even though Bitcoin's supply is capped at 21 million, this scarcity makes even fractional ownership increasingly valuable. For instance, holding just 0.1 or even 0.01 Bitcoin could grow significantly in worth over the coming years, potentially transforming into life-changing wealth for future generations.

Investing in Bitcoin today means providing your children and grandchildren with an asset that will only become rarer and more valuable as demand continues to outpace supply. A decade from now, holding even a small fraction—perhaps just 10% of a Bitcoin—could offer financial security for your grandchildren in a world where Bitcoin is widely accepted as a global standard for value. In this "Bitcoin Utopia," where Bitcoin has cemented itself as a cornerstone of the global financial system, your family's holdings could grow exponentially, allowing them to participate in wealth-building opportunities that are unavailable in traditional fiat-based systems.

By taking action now, you are not merely preserving your own wealth but are setting up a financial legacy that could benefit your family for decades to come. This opportunity to secure generational wealth through Bitcoin may be the single greatest financial decision you can make today.

Bitcoin: A Foundation for Global Prosperity

The concept of a "Bitcoin Utopia" isn't just a future dream—it's a snowball going down a hill. Major institutional players like BlackRock and Fidelity are rapidly accumulating Bitcoin, signaling that the financial revolution driven by Bitcoin is well underway. Since the launch of the first Bitcoin exchange-traded funds (ETFs) in January 2024, BlackRock's iShares Bitcoin Trust (IBIT) has amassed over 119,000 BTC, equivalent to around $6.2 billion by February and continues growing.

By October 2024, the assets under management for BlackRock's Bitcoin ETF have surged to $23.2 billion, making it one of the fastest-growing ETFs in history. Fidelity's Bitcoin ETF has also seen rapid growth, reaching $11 billion in assets.

This institutional demand for Bitcoin, from BlackRock to Fidelity, underscores how valuable Bitcoin is becoming in the global financial system. As these large players continue to acquire Bitcoin, the available supply decreases, driving its scarcity and reinforcing its status as a valuable asset. Additionally, other ETFs combined hold hundreds of thousands of BTC, totaling billions in assets under management.

This financial shift isn't limited to institutional players—nation-states are also starting to recognize Bitcoin's potential. Countries like El Salvador have adopted Bitcoin as legal tender, and more nations are exploring its potential to bypass the reliance on traditional fiat currencies and mitigate issues like inflation or economic instability.

On the adoption front, Bitcoin wallets are increasing rapidly, with millions of new investors joining the network in the past year. The number of Bitcoin wallets has skyrocketed, and as of 2024, there are over 100 million wallets globally, with continued growth fueled by institutional investments and retail interest.

Bitcoin is also driving innovation in how we think about energy use. As more efficient Bitcoin mining practices evolve, Bitcoin can play a role in energy conservation by using surplus energy and creating demand for renewable energy sources. This transformation, combined with Bitcoin's ability to provide financial access to billions of unbanked people worldwide, underscores its potential to create a fairer, more inclusive global economy.

For investors, this is a unique opportunity to be part of a movement that is reshaping the world—both financially and socially. The time to act is now, as institutional and national interest continues to surge, diminishing Bitcoin's already limited supply. By investing in Bitcoin, individuals not only participate in a rapidly appreciating asset but also contribute to building a more transparent, decentralized financial system that benefits humanity as a whole.

The future Bitcoiners envision is not just about revolutionizing finance but about transforming society. In this future, Bitcoin provides a foundation for decentralized governance, financial inclusion, and wealth generation. By allowing individuals to borrow against their Bitcoin holdings at low interest rates, unlocking opportunities for global trade, and providing transparency at every level, Bitcoin has the potential to usher in a new era of global prosperity.

Bitcoin is more than a currency—it's a tool for systemic change, empowering individuals to create wealth, participate in the global economy, and hold powerful entities accountable. The decentralized nature of Bitcoin ensures that power is distributed fairly, and opportunities are abundant for everyone, leading to a more just and equitable world.

A Limited Supply in an Expanding World: Securing Your Share of the Future

The data is clear: Bitcoin is on a trajectory of mass adoption, driven by growing institutional investment and widespread recognition of its role as a store of value. As more countries face the devaluation of their fiat currencies through inflation, debasement, and excessive money printing, individuals across the globe are increasingly searching for a financial safe haven— an asset that preserves the value of their human energy and labor. Bitcoin, with its fixed supply and decentralized nature, is perfectly positioned to fulfill this need.

Bitcoin's capped supply of 21 million ensures that as more institutions, private investors, and even governments acquire and hold it, availability will continue to shrink. This scarcity will drive demand higher, rewarding early adopters who understood its potential. The movement from fiat currencies to Bitcoin is not merely speculative; it's a shift toward a system that promises financial sovereignty, transparency, and protection against inflation. However, time is of the essence. As more Bitcoin is accumulated and locked away by large holders, the window of opportunity narrows.

This moment in history presents a unique chance to secure generational wealth by investing in Bitcoin. As the world begins to realize the flaws of fiat money and the power of decentralized, digital assets, Bitcoin's role as a hedge against economic instability will only strengthen. The time to act is now, as the opportunity to own a piece of this finite asset diminishes with each passing day. By choosing Bitcoin today, individuals are not only investing in a valuable financial asset but also contributing to a future where financial inclusion, transparency, and empowerment are accessible to all.

The future is bright for those who see the potential in Bitcoin and act before its scarcity intensifies. This is not just an investment in wealth but an investment in a new global financial system—one that is decentralized, equitable, and built to last.

Bitcoin Utopia: See you there!

CONCLUSION – A FUTURE POWERED BY BITCOIN

www.ingramcontent.com/pod-product-compliance
Lightning Source LLC
Chambersburg PA
CBHW050318230526
45471CB00005B/2247